WILD DOGS

AN IMAGINATION LIBRARY SERIES

by Victor Gentle and Janet Perry

Gareth Stevens Publishing
A WORLD ALMANAC EDUCATION GROUP COMPANY

Please visit our web site at: www.garethstevens.com
For a free color catalog describing Gareth Stevens Publishing's
list of high-quality books and multimedia programs,
call 1-800-542-2595 or fax your request to (414) 332-3567.

Library of Congress Cataloging-in-Publication Data

Gentle, Victor.
    Dingoes / by Victor Gentle and Janet Perry.
       p. cm. — (Wild dogs: an imagination library series)
    Includes bibliographical references and index.
    Summary: An introduction to the physical characteristics and behavior of the dingo,
also describing its history and impact on the ecosystem in Australia.
    ISBN 0-8368-3096-2 (lib. bdg.)
    1. Dingo—Juvenile literature. [1. Dingo.] I. Perry, Janet. II. Title.
QL737.C22G4467   2002
599.77'2—dc21   2001054949

First published in 2002 by
Gareth Stevens Publishing
A World Almanac Education Group Company
330 West Olive Street, Suite 100
Milwaukee, WI 53212 USA

Text: Victor Gentle and Janet Perry
Page layout: Victor Gentle, Janet Perry, and Tammy Gruenewald
Cover design: Tammy Gruenewald
Series editor: Catherine Gardner
Picture Researcher: Diane Laska-Swanke

Photo credits: Cover (main), pp. 5 (both), 9, 11, 15, 17, 19, 21 © Jean-Paul Ferrero/AUSCAPE;
cover (background) Diane Laska-Swanke; p. 7 © Ken Lucas/Visuals Unlimited; p. 13 © Simon
King/BBC Natural History Unit

Printed in the United States of America

1 2 3 4 5 6 7 8 9 06 05 04 03 02

Front cover: A dingo with a pair of three-month-old pups. Starting as pups, dingoes learn how to show respect to other, stronger, dingoes.

TABLE OF CONTENTS

Words that appear in the glossary are printed in **boldface** type the first time they occur in the text.

THE FENCE

A wire fence snakes its way across Australia. From a cliff on the coast of South Australia, it stretches almost to the Pacific Ocean in Queensland. The fence is 3,307 miles (5,322 kilometers) long.

The fence protects Australia's 115 million sheep from about a million dingoes. It works. Few dingoes are found inside the fence. Wherever dingoes are found, they are trapped and killed, poisoned, or shot.

The main photo shows the dingo fence in New South Wales. In the small photo, a male dingo watches his **pups**. One pup chews on a rabbit.

WHAT IS A DINGO?

Many people think dingoes are pests, but long ago dingoes were pets. From about 6,000 to 10,000 years ago in Asia, wolves began to live with humans. Over thousands of years, pet wolves grew to be different from wild wolves. Dingoes **descended** from the pet wolves.

Later, dingoes returned to the wild. Dingoes now live in Australia and parts of Asia, including Burma and Thailand. Australian dingoes eat meat. They usually are larger than Asian dingoes, which mostly are **vegetarians**.

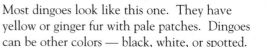

Most dingoes look like this one. They have yellow or ginger fur with pale patches. Dingoes can be other colors — black, white, or spotted.

AUSTRALIA'S TOP DOG

Dingoes first arrived in northern Australia about 3,500 years ago, probably with sailors from Asia. The dingoes spread out and quickly became Australia's top **predator**. Since then, dingoes have killed off at least sixteen **species** of native Australian animals, including other predators, such as the Tasmanian wolf.

Now, dingoes compete with wild cats, which came to Australia as pets about 300 years ago. They also compete with red foxes, which were brought from Europe about 150 years ago.

A dingo works hard for a big snack. Its **prey** is a lace monitor lizard. Lace monitors are not an endangered species, but this one may not escape.

A WAR ON DINGOES

Europeans brought sheep to Australia in the early 1800s. They wanted to use the wool and meat from the sheep, but dingoes found the sheep quite tasty and easy to catch. To protect their sheep, farmers began to kill dingoes. Even today, people can earn money, called a **bounty**, by killing dingoes.

At one time, dingoes helped keep down the number of kangaroos and **wallabies**. Now, inside the fence, people kill thousands of kangaroos to stop them from eating the sheep's grass.

A dingo catches a sheep. Although dingoes are a threat to sheep, they usually hunt sheep only when other food is hard to find.

OUTBACK PACKS

In Australia, most dingoes live in the **outback**, far from humans. There, they form small **packs**, like other wild dogs around the world.

In a pack, dingoes hunt together, share food, and care for each other. Each member of the pack has a job to do. Only the lead male and female have pups. Other pack members — usually pups from the year before — help raise the new pups and hunt.

Some dingoes settle near humans. Usually, these dingoes live alone or with one other dingo and not in packs.

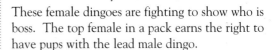

These female dingoes are fighting to show who is boss. The top female in a pack earns the right to have pups with the lead male dingo.

SOUNDING OFF

To work well in a pack, dingoes need good ways to communicate. **Howling** is one way dingoes send messages. They may howl to bond as a pack or to warn other packs to stay away. One dingo might howl to attract another.

A dingo can make other sounds, too. Barks mean "Danger." When a dingo is startled, but not frightened, it snuffs by making short, sharp breaths through its nose. Moans are soft howls used near water holes to tell another pack to leave.

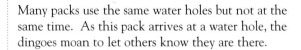

Many packs use the same water holes but not at the same time. As this pack arrives at a water hole, the dingoes moan to let others know they are there.

MAKING SCENTS

Smells, or scents, also help dingoes communicate. To leave scents, dingoes mark small bushes, logs, fence posts, or rocks, and they rake the earth with their claws.

Other dingoes understand these scent messages. Some messages protect a dingo's **territory**. Others help dingoes share information. Some messages tell male dingoes that females are ready to **mate**.

Far from humans, dingoes mark out territories, like wolves, leaving scents on logs and other objects. Here, a dingo patrols its territory.

A PUP'S LIFE

Dingoes have up to ten pups. Mothers **nurse** the pups for eight weeks. Then, the pups try solid snacks like grasshoppers or rabbits. Until the pups learn to hunt, other dingoes in the pack bring them food.

Pups play hard at hunting. First, they practice on pretend prey — their brothers, sisters, and mother. Pretty soon, pups catch their own grasshoppers and rabbits. By the time they are eight months old, pups can feed themselves.

What a big family! This dingo mom has close to the maximum number of pups. How many can you count?

CAN THE DINGO BE SAVED?

Pure dingo pups face a threat. Although at least a million dingoes live in Australia alone, pure dingoes are in danger from **domestic** dogs. Pet dogs, working dogs, and **feral** dogs mate with dingoes. As a result, fewer pure dingoes are left.

Pure dingoes may be gone within fifty years, unless steps are taken to save them. People are concerned, and groups already are at work to save the dingo.

Some groups have encouraged people to keep dingoes as pets. In 1993, the dingo became an official breed and Australia's national dog.

MORE TO READ AND VIEW

Books (Nonfiction) *The Dingo.* Lynn M. Stone (Rourke Corporation)
The Dingo. The Library of Wolves and Dogs (series).
  Janice Koler-Matznick (Powerkids Press)
Wild Dogs (series). Victor Gentle and Janet Perry (Gareth Stevens)
Your Dog's Wild Cousins. Hope Ryden (Penguin Putnam)

Books (Fiction) *The Giant Devil Dingo.* Dick Roughsey (Macmillan)

Books (Activity) *Dogs of the Wild* (coloring book). Peter M. Spizzirri (Spizzirri)

Videos (Nonfiction) *Australia's Dingo Island. Hidden Worlds* (series). (PBS Home Video)
Australia's Kangaroos. (National Geographic)
The Barefoot Bushman. (Goldhil Home Media)
Wild Wonders of Australia. (BFS Video)

Videos (Fiction) *Echo of Thunder.* (Hallmark Hall of Fame)

PLACES TO VISIT, WRITE, OR CALL

Dingoes live at the following zoos. Call or write to the zoos to find out about their dingoes and other wild dogs, or other Australian animals. Better yet, go see the dingoes in person!

The Marion Nature Park
12888 SE US Highway 441
Belleview, FL 34420-4566
(352) 347-7800

Fort Wayne Children's Zoo
3411 Sherman Boulevard
Fort Wayne, IN 46808-1594
(219) 427-6800

The ZOO in Naples
1590 Goodlette-Frank Road
Naples, FL 34102
(941) 262-5409

Kansas City Zoo
Swope Park, 6800 Zoo Drive
Kansas City, MO 64132-4200
(816) 513-5700

22

WEB SITES

If you have your own computer and Internet access, great! If not, most libraries have Internet access. The Internet changes every day, and web sites come and go. We believe the following sites are likely to last and give the best, most appropriate links for readers to find out more about dingoes and other wild dogs around the world.

To get started finding web sites about dingoes, choose a general search engine. You can plug words into the search engine and see what it finds for you. Some words related to dingoes are: *dingo, dingo fence, feral, Australian wildlife, pets, sheep, wild dogs,* and *zoo animals.*

www.yahooligans.com

This is a huge search engine and a great research tool for anything you might want to know. For information on dingoes, click on Animals under the Science & Nature heading. From the Animals page, you can see or hear dingoes and other wild dogs by clicking on Animal Sounds or Animal Pictures.

dmoz.org/Recreation/Pets/Dogs/Wild_Dogs

"*dmoz.org*" gives lists of web sites chosen by a person rather than a search engine. The page given here has a list of web sites (updated from time to time) for wild dogs. Most have photos or diagrams and some are just for kids.

www.dingosanctuary.org

The Australian Native Dog Conservation Society also wants to save dingoes and educate the public. Information, news, stories, and lots of other dingo stuff are here.

www.enchantedlearning.com/Home.html

Type in *dingo* for a simple labeled printout and description of a dingo.

www.thewildones.org

The Wild Ones is a children's site for the Wildlife Trust, which works to help save endangered animals everywhere. Click on Search and type in the word *dingo* to search the web for good kid-friendly sites.

www.wwwins.net.au/dingofarm/001.html

The *Dingo Farm* is dedicated to saving dingoes, and has a great web site full of information, photos, and news about dingoes.

GLOSSARY

You can find these words on the pages listed. Reading a word in a sentence helps you understand it even better.

bounty (BOWN-tee) — price paid to a person for killing a certain kind of animal 10

descended (dih-SEN-did) — to be related to an earlier type of animal 6

domestic (duh-MESS-tik) — kept by humans as pets or to work 20

feral (FIR-uhl) — no longer domestic and now living in the wild 20

howling (HOWL-ing) — making loud cries 14

mate (MAYT) — come together to make babies 16, 20

nurse (NURS) — feed milk to pups 18

outback (OUT-BAK) — land in Australia that is away from towns or cities 12

packs (PAKS) — groups of dingoes 12, 14, 18

predator (PRED-uh-tur) — an animal that hunts other animals for food 8

prey (PRAY) — animals that are hunted by other animals for food 8, 18

pups (PUHPS) — baby dingoes 4, 12, 18, 20

species (SPEE-shees) — a group of plants or animals that are very alike 8

territory (TER-uh-tor-ee) — area of land that an animal (or group of animals) marks out as its hunting ground 16

vegetarians (vej-uh-TER-ee-uhns) — animals that eat only plants for food 6

wallabies (WOL-uh-bees) — Australian animals that look like small kangaroos 10

INDEX